THE USBORNE INTERNET-LINKED
FIRST THOUSAND WORDS
IN JAPANESE

With Internet-linked pronunciation guide

Heather Amery
Illustrated by Stephen Cartwright

Edited by Nicole Irving and Katie Daynes
Designed by Andy Griffin and Hannah Ahmed

Japanese language consultants: Joyce Jenkins,
Tomoko Taguchi-Boyd and Kayoko Yokoyama
With thanks to Terry Shannon

About kana signs

The words in this book are written in simple Japanese signs, called kana. Each kana represents a syllable. (A syllable is part of a word that is a separate sound, for example, "today" has two syllables: "to" and "day".)

Below you can see all the kana signs and find out which sounds they represent. There are also lots of tips to help you make these sounds like a Japanese person.

Japanese has two sets of kana signs, called hiragana and katakana. Hiragana signs are used for the traditional sounds of Japanese. Katakana signs are used for words that Japanese has borrowed from other languages, such as "taoru", borrowed from the English word "towel".

Next to each kana, you can see a guide to how it is said. In the book, each Japanese word is shown in the same way, that is, in kana with a pronunciation guide based on the guides on this page. Japanese also uses more complicated signs, called kanji or "characters". You can find out about kanji on page 56.

Hiragana

あ	a	い	i	う	u	え	e	お	o
か	ka	き	ki	く	ku	け	ke	こ	ko
が	ga	ぎ	gi	ぐ	gu	げ	ge	ご	go
さ	sa	し	shi	す	su	せ	se	そ	so
ざ	za	じ	ji	ず	zu	ぜ	ze	ぞ	zo
た	ta	ち	chi	つ	tsu	て	te	と	to
だ	da			づ	zu	で	de	ど	do
な	na	に	ni	ぬ	nu	ね	ne	の	no
は	ha	ひ	hi	ふ	fu	へ	he	ほ	ho
ば	ba	び	bi	ぶ	bu	べ	be	ぼ	bo
ぱ	pa	ぴ	pi	ぷ	pu	ぺ	pe	ぽ	po
ま	ma	み	mi	む	mu	め	me	も	mo
や	ya			ゆ	yu			よ	yo
ら	ra	り	ri	る	ru	れ	re	ろ	ro
わ	wa							を	(w)o
ん	n								

In the lists above, signs with guides written in slanted letters (like this) are based on the ones

Katakana

ア	a	イ	i	ウ	u	エ	e	オ	o
カ	ka	キ	ki	ク	ku	ケ	ke	コ	ko
ガ	ga	ギ	gi	グ	gu	ゲ	ge	ゴ	go
サ	sa	シ	shi	ス	su	セ	se	ソ	so
ザ	za	ジ	ji	ズ	zu	ゼ	ze	ゾ	zo
タ	ta	チ	chi	ツ	tsu	テ	te	ト	to
ダ	da			ツ	zu	デ	de	ド	do
ナ	na	ニ	ni	ヌ	nu	ネ	ne	ノ	no
ハ	ha	ヒ	hi	フ	fu	ヘ	he	ホ	ho
バ	ba	ビ	bi	ブ	bu	ベ	be	ボ	bo
パ	pa	ピ	pi	プ	pu	ペ	pe	ポ	po
マ	ma	ミ	mi	ム	mu	メ	me	モ	mo
ヤ	ya			ユ	yu			ヨ	yo
ラ	ra	リ	ri	ル	ru	レ	re	ロ	ro
ワ	wa							ヲ	(w)o
ン	n								

above. As you can see, to make this new set of sounds you add a little mark to the kana.

Pronunciation tips

Here are a few tips that will help you to say the kana signs above in a really Japanese way:
· wherever the pronunciation guide shows **a**, say this like the "a" in "father"
· say **i** like the "ee" in "meet"
· say **u** like the "oo" in "cuckoo"
· say **e** like the "e" in "end"
· say **o** like the "o" in "corn"
· when you see a line over a letter (for example **ō**), this shows the sound is long.

For other letters, say them as if they were part of an English word, but remember these tips:
· when you see **r**, say it as a soft "r" sound, halfway between an "l" and an "r"
· when you see **g**, say it as in "garden"
· the **(w)o** sound is shown with the "w" in brackets because you sometimes say "wo", and sometimes just "o". In this book, the pronunciation guide for each word will make clear which sound to make
· the **fu** sound is halfway between "foo" and "hoo"
· the **n** sound on its own (at the bottom of each list) is a nasal "n" sound, much as if you had a cold.

In English, many words have a part that you stress, or say louder. For example, in the word "daisy", you stress "dai". In Japanese, you say each part of the word with the same stress.

On every double page with pictures, there is a little yellow duck to look for. Can you find it?

About this book

This is a great book for anyone starting to learn Japanese, and for anyone who wants to know a bit about the language. You'll find it easy to learn new words by looking at the small, labeled pictures. Then you can practice the words by talking about the large central pictures. This book also has its own Usborne Quicklinks Web site where you can listen to all the Japanese words.

Looking at Japanese words

You will see that Japanese words are written with special signs. You can find out about these on the page opposite and on page 56. It will take you a little time to learn Japanese signs so, to help you, the Japanese word is also written in our alphabet.

Writing in Japanese

Traditionally, Japanese is written from right to left and top to bottom. This means you start a book at what to an American person is the back. In this book, everything is written from left to right, just as in American books.

Saying and listening to Japanese words

Throughout this book you will find an easy how-to-say guide for each Japanese word, but the best way to learn how to speak Japanese is to listen to a Japanese speaker and repeat what you hear. You can listen to all the words in this book, spoken by a Japanese person, on the Usborne Quicklinks Web site. Just go to **www.usborne-quicklinks.com** and type in the keywords "1000 japanese". To hear the words, you will need your Web browser (e.g. Internet Explorer or Netscape Navigator) and a program that lets you play sound (such as RealPlayer® or Windows® Media Player). These programs are free and, if you don't already have one of them, you can download them from Usborne Quicklinks. Your computer also needs a sound card but most computers already have one of these. Please read the **Internet note** for parents and guardians on page 56.

Windows® is a trademark of Microsoft Corporation, registered in the US and other countries.
RealPlayer® is a trademark of RealNetworks, Inc., registered in the US and other countries.

A computer is not essential

If you don't have access to the Internet, don't worry. This book is a complete and excellent Japanese word book on its own.

うち uchi

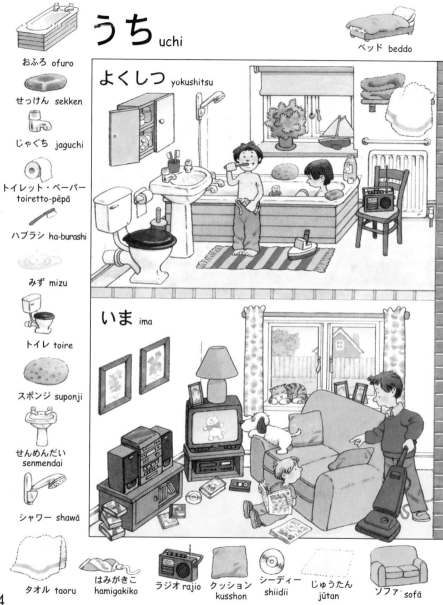

ベッド beddo

おふろ ofuro

せっけん sekken

じゃぐち jaguchi

トイレット・ペーパー
toiretto-pēpā

ハブラシ ha-burashi

みず mizu

トイレ toire

スポンジ suponji

せんめんだい
senmendai

シャワー shawā

よくしつ yokushitsu

いま ima

タオル taoru

はみがきこ
hamigakiko

ラジオ rajio

クッション
kusshon

シーディー
shiidii

じゅうたん
jūtan

ソファ sofā

4

いす isu　かけぶとん kakebuton　くし kushi　シーツ shiitsu　しきもの shikimono　ようふくだんす yōfuku-dansu

しんしつ
shinshitsu

まくら makura

たんす tansu

かがみ kagami

ブラシ burashi

ランプ ranpu

けんかん
genkan

え e

ぼうしかけ bōshi-kake

でんわ denwa

ラジエーター rajiētā　ビデオ bideo　しんぶん shinbun　テーブル tēburu　てがみ tegami　かいだん kaidan

5

だいどころ daidokoro

れいぞうこ reizōko

コップ koppu

とけい tokei

こしかけ koshikake

こさじ kosaji

スイッチ suitchi

せんざい senzai

かぎ kagi

ドア doa

そうじき sōjiki

ながし nagashi

なべ nabe

フォーク fōku

エプロン epuron

アイロンだい airon-dai

ごみ gomi

6

やかん yakan

ナイフ naifu

モップ moppu

はたき hataki

タイル tairu

ほうき hōki

せんたくき sentakuki

ちりとり chiritori

ひきだし hikidashi

うけざら ukezara

フライパン furaipan

レンジ renji

スプーン supūn

おさら osara

アイロン airon

ふきん fukin

コーヒーカップ kōhii-kappu

マッチ matchi

たわし tawashi

おわん owan

たな tana

にわ niwa

ておしいちりんしゃ
te-oshi-ichirinsha

みつばちのす
mitsubachi no su

やかん
katatsumuri

れんが renga

はと hato

すき suki

てんとうむし
tentō-mushi

ごみいれ gomi-ire

たね tane

こや koya

じょうろ jōro

みみず mimizu

はな hana

ごみいれ
supurinkurā

くわ kuwa

すずめばち
suzume-bachi

みつばち mitsubachi

シャベル shaberu

ほね hone

かきね kakine

またぐわ mataguwa

しばかりき shibakariki

こみち ko-michi

は ha

き ki

けむり kemuri

けむし kemushi

くまで kumade

とりのす tori no su

ぼう bō

くさ kusa

うばぐるま ubaguruma

はしご hashigo

たきび takibi

ホース hōsu

おんしつ onshitsu

9

さぎょうば sagyōba

まんりき manriki

かみやすり kami-yasuri

ドリル doriru

はしご hashigo

のこぎり nakogiri

おがくず ogakuzu

カレンダー karendā

どうぐばこ dōgu-bako

スクリュードライバー sukuryū-doraibā

いた ita

かんなくず kanna-kuzu

ペンナイフ pen-naifu

ねじ neji

10

びょう byō   くも kumo   ボルト boruto   おやねじ oya-neji   くものす kumo no su

たる taru

はえ hae

おの ono

まきじゃく makijaku

ハンマー hanmā

やすり yasuri

かんペンキ kan-penki

ざいもく zaimoku   くぎ kugi   さぎょうだい sagyōdai   びん bin   かんな kanna

11

とおり tōri

みせ mise

あな ana

きっさてん kissaten

きゅうきゅうしゃ
kyūkyūsha

ほどう hodō

アンテナ antena

えんとつ entotsu

やね yane

しゅんせつき
shunsetsuki

ホテル hoteru

バス basu

おとこ otoko

パトカー patokā

パイプ paipu

ドリル doriru

がっこう gakkō

うんどうじょう undō-jō

タクシー takushii

おうだんほどう ōdan-hodō

こうじょう kōjō

トラック torakku

こうつうしんごう kōtsū-shingō

えいがかん eiga-kan

ライトバン raito-ban

ローラー rōrā

トレーラー torērā

いえ ie

いちば ichiba

ふみだん fumidan

オートバイ ōtobai

じてんしゃ jitensha

しょうぼうしゃ shōbō-sha

けいかん keikan

くるま kuruma

おんな onna

がいとう gaitō

アパート apāto

13

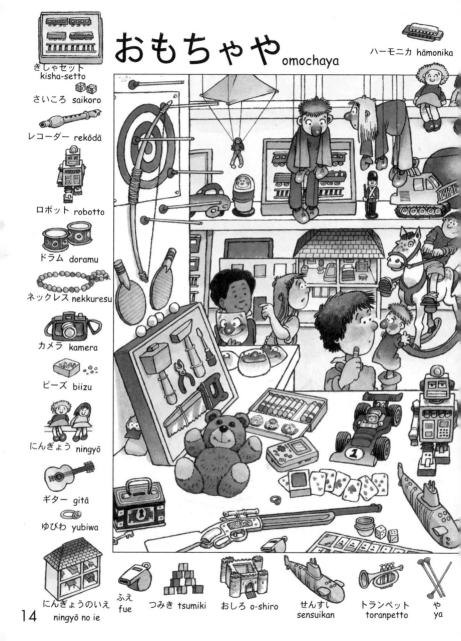

おもちゃや omochaya

ハーモニカ hāmonika

きしゃセット kisha-setto

さいころ saikoro

レコーダー rekōdā

ロボット robotto

ドラム doramu

ネックレス nekkuresu

カメラ kamera

ビーズ biizu

にんぎょう ningyō

ギター gitā

ゆびわ yubiwa

にんぎょうのいえ ningyō no ie

ふえ fue

つみき tsumiki

おしろ o-shiro

せんすい sensuikan

トランペット toranpetto

や ya

ゆみ yumi

ハーモニカ parashūto

ボート bōto

フェイスペイント fueisu-peinto

ローラー rōrā

おめん omen

レーシングカー rēshingu-kā

もくば mokuba

ちょきんばこ chokin-bako

ビーだま bii-dama

あやつりにんぎょう ayatsuri-ningyō

ピアノ piano

うちゅうひこうし uchū-hikōshi

クレーン kurēn

ねんど nendo

てっぽう teppō

へいたい heitai

えのぐ enogu

ロケット roketto

15

こうえん kōen

ぶらんこ buranko

ベンチ benchi

すなば sunaba

ピクニック pikunikku

たこ tako

アイスクリーム
aisukuriimu

いぬ inu

もん mon

こみち ko-michi

かえる kaeru

すべりだい
suberidai

おたまじゃくし
otamajakushi

いけ ike

ローラースケート rōrā-sukēto

やぶ yabu

16

あかんぼう akanbō

スケートボード sukētobōdo

つち tsuchi

ておしぐるま te-oshi-guruma

シーソー shiisō

こども kodomo

さんりんしゃ sanrinsha

とり tori

さく saku

まり mari

ヨット yotto

いと ito

みずたまり mizu-tamari

こがも ko-gamo

なわとび nawatobi

かだん kadan

はくちょう hakuchō

ひきひも hikihimo

かも kamo

き ki

17

どうぶつえん dōbutsuen

つばさ tsubasa

わし washi

かば kaba

パンダ panda

まえあし mae-ashi

ゴリラ gorira

カンガルー kangarū

こうもり kōmori

さる saru

ひょうざん hyōzan

ペンギン pengin

しっぽ shippo

おおかみ ōkami

わに wani

くま kuma

はね hane

ペリカン perikan

だちょう dachō

イルカ iruka

ライオン raion

ようじゅう yōjū

キリン kirin

18

つの tsuno

しか shika

らくだ rakuda

あざらし azarashi

しろくま shiro-kuma

かめ kame

ぞうのはな zō no hana

さい sai

ぞう zō

やぎゅう yagyū

ビーバー biibā

やぎ yagi

しまうま shima-uma

へび hebi

さめ same

くじら kujira

とら tora

ひょう hyō

19

せんろ senro

りょこう ryokō

エンジン enjin

かんしょうき kanshōki

きゃくしゃ kyakusha

うんてんしゅ untenshu

かしゃ kasha

プラットフォーム puratto-hōmu

しゃしょう shashō

スーツケース sūtsukēsu

じょうしゃけんはんばいき jōshaken-hanbaiki

ヘリコプター herikoputā

えき eki

ガソリンスタンド gasorin-sutando

20

しんごう shingō

リュックサック rukkusakku

ヘッドライト heddo-raito

エンジン enjin

しゃりん sharin

でんち denchi

ひこうき hikōki

スチュワーデス suchuwādesu

かっそうろ kassōro

かんせいとう kanseitō

ひこうじょう hikōjō

スチュワード suchuwādo

パイロット pairotto

せんしゃ sensha

トランク toranku

ガソリン gasorin

レッカーしゃ rekkā-sha

せんしゃ

ガソリンポンプ gasorin-ponpu

ガソリンタンクローリー gasorin-tankurōrii

スパナ supana

タイヤ taiya

ボンネット bonnetto

オイル oiru

いなか inaka

ふうしゃごや
fūsha-goya

ねつききゅう
netsu-kikyū

ちょうちょ
chō-chō

とかげ tokage

いし ishi

きつね kitsune

おがわ ogawa

みちしるべ
michi-shirube

ちょうちょ
hari-nezumi

やま yama

すいもん sui-mon　りす risu　もり mori　あなぐま anaguma　かわ kawa　みち michi

22

テント tento

 うんが unga

 まるた maruta

 むら mura

が ga

 はし hashi

 はしけ hashike

 たき taki

 ふくろう fukurō

 トンネル tonneru

 こぎつね kogitsune

 もぐら mogura

 つりびと tsuri-bito

いわ iwa

ひきがえる hikigaeru

でんしゃ densha

キャンピングカー kyanpingu-kā

 おか oka

23

のうじょう nōjō

ほしくさのやま
hoshikusa no yama

ぼくようけん
bokuyō-ken

あひる ahiru

こひつじ ko-hitsuji

いけ ike

ひよこ hiyoko

やねうら yane-ura

ぶたごや buta-goya

おうし o-ushi

あひるのこ ahiru no ko

にわとりごや
niwatori-goya

おんどり ondori

24 トラクター torakutā がちょう gachō タンクしゃ tanku-sha なや naya ぬかるみ nukarumi　ておしぐるま te-oshi-guruma

のうふ nōfu

そうげん sōgen

めんどり mendori

こうし ko-ushi

へい hei

サドル sadoru

うしごや ushi-goya

めうし me-ushi

すき suki

うまごや kaju

うまごや uma-goya

こぶた ko-buta

ひつじかい hitsujikai

しちめんちょう shichimenchō

かかし kakashi

ほしくさ hoshi-kusa

ひつじ hitsuji

わらたば wara-taba

うま uma

ぶた buta

のうか nōka

25

はんせん hansen

うみ umi

オール ōru

とうだい tōdai

シャベル shaberu

バケツ baketsu

ひとで hitode

すなのしろ suna no shiro

ビーチパラソル biichi-parasoru

はた hata

せんいん senin

うみべ umibe

かい kai

かに kani   かもめ kamome   しま shima   モーターボート mōtā-bōtō   すいじょうスキー suijō-sukii

26

なみ nami
なつのぼうし natsu no bōshi
がけ gake
ふね fune
カヌー kanū
ロープ rōpu

こいし koishi
かいそう kaisō
あみ ami
みずかき mizu-kaki
つりぶね tsuri-bune
あしびれ ashi-bire
ろば roba
さかな sakana

みずぎ mizugi
オイルタンカー oiru-tankā
はまべ hamabe
ボート bōto
おりたたみいす oritatami-isu

27

はさみ hasami

けいさん keisan

けしごむ keshigomu

ものさし monosashi

しゃしん shashin

フェルトペン
fueruto-pen

がびょう gabyō

えのぐ enogu

おとこのこ
otoko no ko

えんぴつ enpitsu

がっこう_{gakkō}

こくばん kokuban

つくえ tsukue

ほん hon

ペン pen

のり nori

チョーク chōku

え e

ごみばこ gomibako
せんせい sensei
はこ hako
ちず chizu
ふで fude
てんじょう tenjō
かべ kabe
ゆか yuka
ノート nōto
アルファベット arufabetto
バッジ bajji
すいそう suisō
かみ kami
ブラインド buraindo
ドアのとって doa no totte
しょくぶつ shokubutsu
ちきゅうぎ chikyūgi
おんなのこ onna no ko
クレヨン kureyon
スタンド sutando
イーゼル iizeru

a b c d e f g
h i j k l m n
o p q r s t u
v w x y z

29

かんごふ kangofu

だっしめん
dasshimen

くすり kusuri

エレベーター erebētā

ガウン gaun

まつばづえ
matsuba-zue

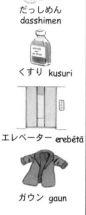

じょうざい jōzai

おぼん o-bon

うでとけい
ude-dokei

たいおんけい
taionkei

カーテン kāten

びょういん byōin

テディベア
tedibea

りんご
ringo

30

ギプス
gibusu

ほうたい hōtai

くるまいす
kuruma-isu

ジグゾーパズル
jiguzō-pazuru

いしゃ isha

ちゅうしゃき
chūshaki

いしゃ isha

スリッパ surippa

コンピューター konpyūtā

バンドエイド bando-eido

バナナ banana

ぶどう budō

かご kago

おもちゃ omocha

なし nashi

カード kādo

おむつ omutsu

つえ tsue

テレビ terebi

ねまき nemaki

パジャマ pajama

オレンジ orenji

ティッシュ・ペーパー tisshu-pēpā

まんが manga

まちあいしつ machiai-shitsu

31

パーティー pātii

プレゼント purezento

ふうせん fūsen

チョコレート
chokorēto

おかし okashi

まど mado

はなび hanabi

リボン ribon

ケーキ kēki

ストロー
sutorō

ろうそく
rōsoku

かみくさり kami-kusari

おもちゃ omocha

みかん mikan

サラミ sarami

カセットテープ kasetto-tēpu

ソーセージ sōsēji

ポテトチップス poteto-chippusu

かそうふく kasō-fuku

さくらんぼ sakuranbo

フルーツジュース furūtsu-jūsu

きいちご ki-ichigo

いちご ichigo

でんきゅう denkyū

サンドウィッチ sandoitchi

バター batā

ビスケット bisuketto

チーズ chiizu

パン pan

テーブルクロス tēburu-kurosu

33

グレープフルーツ
gurēpu-furūtsu

おみせ omise

かいものぶくろ
kaimono-bukuro

にんじん ninjin

カリフラワー
karifurawā

にら nira

マッシュルーム
masshurūmu

きゅうり kyūri

レモン remon

セロリ serori

アプリコット
apurikotto

チーズ

くだもの と やさい

メロン
meron

たまねぎ
tamanegi

キャベツ
kyabetsu

もも momo

レタス retasu

さやえんどう
saya-endō

トマト
tomato

たまご tamago

プラム puramu

こむぎこ komugiko

はかり hakari

びん bin

にく niku

パイン pain

ヨーグルト yōguruto

バスケット basuketto

ボトル botoru

ハンドバッグ hando-baggu

さいふ saifu

おかね o-kane

かんづめ kanzume

じゃがいも jaga-imo

ほうれんそう hōrensō

いんげん ingen

レジ reji

かぼちゃ kabocha

トロリー tororii

35

たべもの tabemono

ひるごはん hiru-gohan

あさごはん asa-gohan

ゆでたまご yude-tamago

トースト tōsuto

ジャム jamu

コーヒー kōhii

めだまやき medama-yaki

クリーム kuriimu

ぎゅうにゅう gyūnyū

コーンフレーク kōn-furēku

ココア kokoa

さとう satō

はちみつ hachimitsu

しお shio

こしょう koshō

こうちゃ kōcha

ティーポット tiipotto

ホットケーキ hotto-kēki

ロールパン rōru-pan

36

ばんごはん ban-gohan

ハム hamu

スープ sūpu

オムレツ omuretsu

はし hashi

サラダ sarada

ハンバーガー hanbāgā

とりにく tori-niku

ごはん gohan

ソース sōsu

スパゲッティー supagettii

マッシュポテト masshu-poteto

ピザ piza

フライドポテト furaido-poteto

デザート dezāto

37

わたし watashi

あたま atama

かみ kami

かお kao

まゆげ mayuge

め me

はな hana

ほほ hoho

くち kuchi

くちびる kuchibiru

は ha

した shita

あご ago

うで ude

ひじ hiji

おなか onaka

みみ mimi

くび kubi

かた kata

つまさき tsumasaki

あし ashi

あし ashi

ひざ hiza

むね mune

せなか senaka

おしり oshiri

て te

おやゆび oya-yubi

ゆび yubi

38

わたしのようふく watashi no yōfuku

ソックス sokkusu

パンツ pantsu

ランニングシャツ ranning-shatsu

ズボン zubon

ジーパン jiipan

ティーシャツ tiishatsu

スカート sukāto

シャツ shatsu

ネクタイ nekutai

はんズボン hanzubon

タイツ taitsu

ドレス doresu

ジャンパー janpā

トレーナー torēnā

カーディガン kādigan

スカーフ sukāfu

ハンカチ hankachi

スニーカー suniikā

くつ kutsu

サンダル sandaru

ブーツ būtsu

てぶくろ tebukuro

ベルト beruto

バックル bakkuru

ジッパー jippā

くつひも kutsuhimo

ボタン botan

ボタンのあな botan no ana

ポケット poketto

コート kōto

ジャケット jaketto

やきゅうぼう yakyū-bō

ぼうし bōshi

39

ひと hito

だんゆう danyū   じょゆう joyū

コック kokku

ダンサー dansā

かしゅ kashu

うちゅうひこうし uchū-hikōshi

けいかん keikan   ふじんけいかん fujin-keikan

にくや nikuya

だいく daiku

しょうぼうし shōbōshi

がか gaka

さいばんかん saibankan

せいびし seibishi

びょうし biyōshi

トラックのうんてんしゅ
torakku no untenshu

バスのうんてんしゅ
basu no untenshu

ウェイター
ueitā

ウェイトレス
ueitoresu

ゆうびんはいたつにん
yūbin-haitatsunin

はいしゃ haisha

せんすいふ sensuifu

ペンキや penkiya

パンや panya

かぞく kazoku

むすこ
musuko
おとうと
otōto

むすめ
musume
あね
ane

はは haha
つま tsuma

ちち chichi
おっと otto

おば oba

おじ oji

いとこ itoko

そふ
sofu

そぼ sobo

41

どうさ dōsa

わらう warau

ほほえむ hohoemu

なく naku

かんがえる kangaeru

きく kiku

うけとる uketoru

なげる nageru

こわす kowasu

えがく egaku

かく kaku

たたききる tataki-kiru

きる kiru

たべる taberu

はなす hanasu

ほる horu

はこぶ hakobu

のむ nomu

つくる tsukuru

とぶ tobu

はう hau

おどる odoru

あらう arau

あむ amu

みる miru

のぼる noboru

あそぶ asobu

とる toru

はねる haneru

けんかする kenka-suru

ねる neru

ぬう nuu

まつ matsu

りょうりする ryōri-suru

かくれる kakureru

ぬう yomu

かう kau

おす osu

うたう utau

ふく fuku

ひく hiku

はく haku

つむ tsumu

ころぶ korobu

あるく aruku

はしる hashiru

すわる suwaru

43

はんたいのことば
hantai no kotoba

とおい tōi

ちかい chikai

よい yoi

わるい warui

いちばんうえ ichiban-ue

つめたい tsumetai　あつい atsui

ちかい nureru

かわいてる kawaiteru

いちばんした ichiban-shita

きたない kitanai　きれい kirei

うえ ue

した shita

ふとった futotta　やせた yaseta

あく aku　　しまる shimaru

ちいさい chiisai　おおきい ōkii

すくない sukunai

おおい ōi

いちばん ichiban　さいご saigo

ひだり hidari

そと soto

なか naka

かんたん kantan

むずかしい muzukashii

から kara

いっぱい ippai

やわらかい yawarakai

かたい katai

まえ mae

たかい takai

おそい osoi

はやい hayai

うしろ ushiro

ひくい hikui

ながい nagai

みじかい mijikai

かれた kareta

さいている saiteiru

くらい kurai

あかるい akarui

ふるい furui

にかい nikai

みぎ migi

あたらしい atarashii

いっかい ikkai

45

いろいろなひ iroirona-hi

にちようび
nichi-yōbi

もくようび
moku-yōbi

かようび
ka-yōbi

すいようび
sui-yōbi

どようび
do-yōbi

げつようび
getsu-yōbi

きんようび
kin-yōbi

カレンダー
karendā

あさ asa

ゆうがた yūgata

たいよう taiyō

よる yoru

うちゅう uchū

わくせい
wakusei

うちゅうせん
uchū-sen

つき tsuki

ほし hoshi

てんたいぼうえんきょう
tentai-bōenkyō

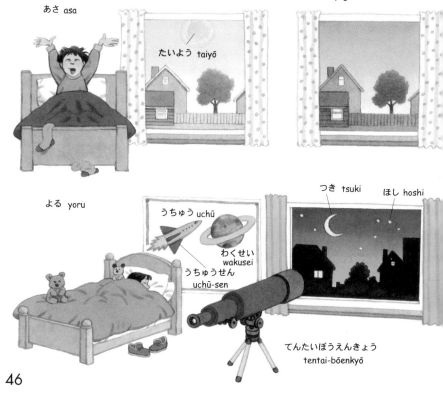

46

とくべつなひ tokubetsuna-hi

たんじょうび
tanjōbi

たんじょうびのカード
tanjōbi no kādo

ろうそく rōsoku

きゅうか kyūka

プレゼント
purezento

たんじょうびのケーキ
tanjōbi no kēki

けっこんしき kekkon-shiki

カメラ kamera

ブライズ・メイド
buraizu meido

はなよめ
hana-yome

はなむこ
hana-muko

カメラマン
kamera-man

クリスマス kurisumasu

トナカイ
tonakai

そり sori

サンタクロース santa-kurōsu

クリスマスツリー
kurisumasu-tsurii

47

てんき tenki

たいよう taiyō

くも kumo

かさ kasa

そら sora

あめ ame

きり kiri

かみなり kaminari

ゆき yuki

つゆ tsuyu

かぜ kaze

かすみ kasumi

しも shimo

にじ niji

きせつ kisetsu

はる haru

なつ natsu

あき aki

ふゆ fuyu

48

ペット petto

じゅうい jūi

ハムスター hamusutā

いぬごや inu-gora

モルモット morumotto

いぬ inu

こいぬ ko-inu

てのりぶんちょう tenori-bunchō

おうむ ōmu

くちばし kuchibashi

えさ esa

カナリア kanaria

うさぎ usagi

とりかご torikago

ねこ neko

バスケット basuketto

ねずみ nezumi

こねこ ko-neko

ぎゅうにゅう gyūnyū

きんぎょ kingyo

49

スポーツとうんどう supōtsu to undō

ボートのり bōto-nori

スノウボード sunō-bōdo

セーリング sēringu

ウィンドサーフィン uindo-sāfin

クリケット kuriketto

からて karate

バスケットボール basuketto-bōru

ラケット raketto

バット batto

ボール bōru

たいそう taisō

テニス tenisu

アメリカンフットボール amerikan-futtobōru

つりざお tsuri-zao

ダンス dansu

やきゅう yakyū

えさ esa

つり tsuri

ラグビー ragubii

とびこみ tobikomi

プール pūru

すいえい suiei

レース rēsu

50

アーチェリー ācherii

まと mato

ハングライダー hanguraidā

ヘルメット herumetto

ジョギング jogingu

じてんしゃ jitensha

ロッククライミング rokku-karaimingu

じゅうどう jūdō

ロッカー rokkā

うま uma

こうま ko-uma

サッカー sakkā

じょうば jōba

こういしつ kōi-shitsu

バトミントン batominton

たっきゅう takkyū

スケートぐつ sukēto-gutsu

アイススケート aisu-sukēto

ストック sutokku

スキーリフト sukii-rifuto

スキーいた sukii-ita

スキー sukii

すもう sumō

51

いろ iro

だいだいいろ daidai-iro

みどり midori

くろ kuro

はいいろ hai-iro

あか aka

ちゃいろ cha-iro

しろ shiro　　あお ao

ピンク pinku

むらさき murasaki

きいろ ki-iro

かたち katachi

ちょうほうけい chōhōkei

えん en

ひしがた hishigata

コーン kōn

ほし hoshi

りっぽうたい rippōtai

だえんけい daenkei

さんかくけい sankakukei

せいほうけい seihōkei

みかづき mikazuki

52

かず kazu

1 いち ichi

2 に ni

3 さん san

4 し shi

5 ご go

6 ろく roku

7 しち shichi

8 はち hachi

9 きゅう kyū

10 じゅう jū

11 じゅういち jūichi

12 じゅうに jūni

13 じゅうさん jūsan

14 じゅうし jūshi

15 じゅうご jūgo

16 じゅうろく jūroku

17 じゅうしち jūshichi

18 じゅうはち jūhachi

19 じゅうきゅう jūkyū

20 にじゅう nijū

ゆうえんち yūenchi

メリーゴーランド merii-gō-rando

マット matto

すべりだい suberidai

かんらんしゃ karansha

おばけやしき obake-yashiki

ポップコーン poppu-kōn

わなげ wanage

ジェットコースター jetto-kōsutā

しゃげき shageki

ゴーカート gō-kāto

わたあめ wata-ame

サーカス sākasu

つなわたり tsunawatari

ボール pōru

くうちゅうブランコ kuchū-buranko

ワイヤーロープ waiyā-rōpu

なわばしご nawabashigo

いちりんしゃのり ichirinsha-nori

あんぜんネット anzen-netto

うさぎ usagi

アクロバット akurabatto

ちょうきょうし chōkyōshi

いぬ inu

フープ fūpu

きょくげいし kyokugeishi

シルクハット shiruku-hatto

ちょうねくたい chō-nekutai

バンド bando

うまのり umanori

ピエロ piero

55

About *kanji*

The Japanese signs used in this book (see page two) are called *kana*, and they are based on sounds. They are simple signs that you use when you first learn Japanese. Normally, they are used mixed in with some other, more complicated signs, called *kanji* or "characters". Each *kanji* represents a word or an idea.

When people first started to write, they used simple pictures of things to show what they were writing about. This is how *kanji* started, and some *kanji* signs still look like what they represent. For example: 木 this *kanji* means "tree". It can also be written using *kana*, き, and said as "ki". 森 this *kanji* means "forest". Notice that it is made from three "tree" *kanji*.

There are many *kanji*. To read a newspaper, you have to know around 2000. It takes a few years to learn them, so it is best to start with *kana*, learning a few of these at a time.

About the word list

In this list, you can find all the Japanese words in the book. For each double page, the Japanese words are shown written in our alphabet. Next to each word you can see its translation (what it means in English).

The translations match the pictures, so if the picture shows leaves, the translation is "leaves", not "leaf". In Japanese, though, there is usually no difference between singular and plural (one and many), so "leaf" and "leaves" are both "ha".

To know how you should say the Japanese words, look at page two or go to the Usborne Quicklinks Web site at **www.usborne-quicklinks.com** and type in the keywords "1000 japanese". There you can listen to all the words in this book, spoken by a native Japanese person.

Internet note for parents and guardians

Please ensure that your children read and follow the Internet safety guidelines displayed on the Usborne Quicklinks Web site.

The links in Usborne Quicklinks are regularly reviewed and updated. However, the content of a Web site may change at any time and Usborne Publishing is not responsible for the content on any Web site other than its own. We recommend that children are supervised while on the Internet, that they do not use Internet Chat Rooms, and that you use Internet filtering software to block unsuitable material. For more information, see the **Net Help** area on the Usborne Quicklinks Web site.

---

pages 4-5

uchi	**home**
yokushitsu	**bathroom**
ofuro	bathtub
sekken	soap
jaguchi	faucet
toiretto-pēpā	toilet paper
ha-burashi	toothbrush
mizu	water
toire	toilet
suponji	sponge
senmendai	sink
shawā	shower
taoru	towel
hamigakiko	toothpaste
rajio	radio
ima	**living room**
kusshon	cushion
shiidii	CD
jūtan	carpet
sofā	sofa
rajiētā	radiator
bideo	video
genkan	**hall**
shinbun	newspaper
tēburu	table
tegami	letters
kaidan	stairs
denwa	telephone
bōshi-kake	hat pegs
shinshitsu	**bedroom**
e	pictures
ranpu	lamp
burashi	brush
kagami	mirror
tansu	chest of drawers
makura	pillow
yōfuku-dansu	wardrobe
shikimono	rug
shiitsu	sheet
kushi	comb
kakebuton	comforter
isu	chair
beddo	bed

pages 6-7

daidokoro	**kitchen**
reizōko	refrigerator
koppu	cups
tokei	clock
koshikake	stool
kosaji	teaspoons
suitchi	light switch
senzai	laundry detergent
kagi	key
doa	door
sōjiki	vacuum cleaner
nabe	saucepans
fōku	forks
epuron	apron
airon-dai	ironing board
gomi	trash
fukin	dish towel
kōhii-kappu	coffee cups
matchi	matches
tawashi	scrub brush
owan	bowls
tana	cupboard
airon	iron
osara	plates
supūn	spoons
renji	cooker
furaipan	frying pan
ukezara	saucers
hikidashi	drawer
chiritori	dustpan
sentakuki	washing machine
hōki	broom
tairu	tiles
hataki	dust cloth
moppu	mop
naifu	knives
yakan	kettle
nagashi	sink

pages 8-9

niwa	**garden**
te-oshi-ichirinsha	wheelbarrow
mitsubachi no su	beehive
katatsumuri	snail
renga	bricks
hato	pigeon
suki	spade
tentō-mushi	ladybug
gomi-ire	trash can
tane	seeds
koya	shed
mimizu	worm
hana	flowers
supurinkurā	sprinkler
kuwa	hoe
suzume-bachi	wasp
kusa	grass
ubaguruma	baby buggy
hashigo	ladder
takibi	bonfire
hōsu	hose
onshitsu	greenhouse
bō	sticks
tori no su	bird's nest
kumade	rake
kemushi	caterpillar
kemuri	smoke
ki	tree
ha	leaves
ko-michi	path
shibakariki	lawn mower
mataguwa	fork
kakine	hedge
hone	bone
shaberu	trowel
mitsubachi	honeybee
jōro	watering can

pages 10-11

sagyōba	**workshop**
manriki	vise
kami-yasuri	sandpaper
doriru	drill
hashigo	ladder
nokogiri	saw
ogakuzu	sawdust
karendā	calendar
dogū-bako	toolbox
sukuryū-doraibā	screwdriver
ita	plank
kanna-kuzu	wood shavings
pen-naifu	pocketknife
zaimoku	wood

kugi	nails
sagyōdai	workbench
bin	jars
kanna	wood plane
kan-penki	paint can
yasuri	file
hanmā	hammer
makijaku	tape measure
ono	ax
hae	fly
taru	barrel
kumo no su	cobweb
oya-neji	nuts
boruto	bolts
kumo	spider
byō	tacks
neji	screws

pages 12-13

tōri	**street**
mise	store
ana	hole
kissaten	café
kyūkyūsha	ambulance
hodō	sidewalk
antena	(TV) antenna
entotsu	chimney
yane	roof
shunsetsuki	digger
hoteru	hotel
otoko	man
patokā	police car
paipu	pipes
doriru	drill
gakkō	school
undō-jō	playground
jitensha	bicycle
shōbō-sha	fire engine
keikan	policeman
kuruma	car
onna	woman
gaitō	lamp post
apāto	apartments
ōtobai	motorcycle
fumidan	steps
ichiba	market
ie	house
tōrerā	trailer
rōrā	steamroller

raito-ban	van
eiga-kan	movie theater
kōtsū-shingō	traffic lights
torakku	truck
kōjō	factory
ōdan-hodō	crosswalk
takushii	taxi
basu	bus

pages 14-15

omochaya	**toy shop**
kisha-setto	train set
saikoro	dice
rekōdā	recorder
robotto	robot
doramu	drums
nekkuresu	necklace
kamera	camera
biizu	beads
ningyō	dolls
gitā	guitar
yubiwa	ring
ningyō no ie	doll's house
fue	whistle
tsumiki	blocks
o-shiro	castle
sensuikan	submarine
toranpetto	trumpet
yane	arrows
kurēn	crane
nendo	clay
teppō	gun
heitai	soldiers
enogu	paints
roketto	rocket
uchū-hikōshi	spacemen
piano	piano
ayatsuri-ningyō	puppets
bii-dama	marbles
chokin-bako	money box
mokuba	rocking horse
rēshingu-kā	racing car
omen	masks
rōrā	steamroller
fueisu-peinto	face paints
bōto	boat
parashūto	parachute
yumi	bow
hāmonika	harmonica

pages 16-17

koēn	**park**
buranko	swings
sunaba	sandbox
pikunikku	picnic
tako	kite
aisukuriimu	ice cream
inu	dog
mon	gate
ko-michi	path
kaeru	frog
suberidai	slide
otamajakushi	tadpoles
ike	lake
rōrā-sukēto	roller skates
yabu	bush
kadan	flower bed
hakuchō	swans
hikihimo	dog leash
kamo	ducks
ki	trees
nawatobi	jump rope
ko-gamo	ducklings
mizu-tamari	puddle
ito	string
yotto	yacht
mari	ball
saku	fence
tori	birds
sanrinsha	tricycle
kodomo	children
shiisō	seesaw
te-oshi-guruma	stroller
tsuchi	dirt
sukētobōdo	skateboard
akanbō	baby
benchi	bench

pages 18-19

dōbutsuen	**zoo**
panda	panda
washi	eagle
tsubasa	wing
kaba	hippopotamus
kōmori	bat
gorira	gorilla
kangarū	kangaroo
mae-ashi	(front) paws

saru	monkey
shippo	tail
ōkami	wolf
wani	crocodile
pengin	penguin
hyōzan	iceberg
kuma	bear
perikan	pelican
dachō	ostrich
hane	feathers
iruka	dolphin
kirin	giraffe
raion	lion
yōjū	lion cubs
shika	deer
tsuno	antlers
rakuda	camel
azarashi	seal
shiro-kuma	polar bear
kame	tortoise
zō	elephant
zō no hana	trunk
sai	rhinoceros
yagyū	buffalo
yagi	goat
shima-uma	zebra
same	shark
biibā	beaver
hebi	snake
kujira	whale
tora	tiger
hyō	leopard

pages 20-21

ryokō	**travel**
eki	**station**
senro	train track
enjin	engine
kanshōki	buffers
kyakusha	railway cars
untenshu	train engineer
kasha	freight train
puratto-hōmu	platform
shashō	ticket inspector
sūtsukēsu	suitcase
jōshaken-hanbaiki	ticket machine
shingō	signals
ryukkusakku	backpack

gasorin-sutando	**gas station**
heddo-raito	headlights
enjin	engine
sharin	wheel
denchi	battery
gasorin-tankurōrii	oil tanker
supana	wrench
taiya	tire
bonnetto	hood (car)
oiru	oil
gasorin-ponpu	gas pump
rekkā-sha	tow truck
gasorin	gasoline
toranku	trunk (car)
sensha	car wash
hikōjō	**airport**
pairotto	pilot
suchuwādo	(male) flight attendant
kanseitō	control tower
kassōro	runway
suchuwādesu	(female) flight attendant
hikōki	plane
herikoputā	helicopter

pages 22-23

inaka	**country**
fūsha-goya	windmill
netsu-kikyū	hot-air balloon
chō-cho	butterfly
tokage	lizard
ishi	stones
kitsune	fox
ogawa	stream
michi-shirube	signpost
hari-nezumi	hedgehog
sui-mon	lock (canal)
risu	squirrel
mori	forest
anaguma	badger
kawa	river
michi	road
iwa	rocks
hikigaeru	toad
densha	train
kyanpingu-kā	camper
oka	hill
tsuri-bito	fisherman

mogura	mole
kogitsune	fox cubs
tonneru	tunnel
fukurō	owl
taki	waterfall
hashike	barge
hashi	bridge
ga	moth
mura	village
maruta	logs
unga	canal
tento	tents
yama	mountain

pages 24-25

nōjō	**farm**
hoshikusa no yama	haystack
bokuyō-ken	sheepdog
ahiru	ducks
ko-hitsuji	lambs
ike	pond
hiyoko	chicks
yane-ura	loft
buta-goya	pigsty
o-ushi	bull
ahiru no ko	ducklings
niwatori-goya	hen house
torakutā	tractor
gachō	geese
tanku-sha	tanker
naya	barn
nukarumi	mud
te-oshi-guruma	cart
hoshi-kusa	hay
hitsuji	sheep
wara-taba	straw bales
uma	horse
buta	pigs
nōka	farmhouse
kakashi	scarecrow
shichimenchō	turkeys
hitsujikai	shepherdess
ko-buta	piglets
uma-goya	stable
kaju	orchard
suki	plow
me-ushi	cow
ushi-goya	cowshed

sadoru	saddle
hei	fence
ko-ushi	calf
mendori	hens
sōgen	field
nōfu	farmer
ondori	rooster

pages 26-27

umibe	**seaside**
hansen	sailboat
umi	sea
ōru	oar
tōdai	lighthouse
shaberu	spade
baketsu	bucket
hitode	starfish
suna no shiro	sandcastle
biichi-parasoru	beach umbrella
hata	flag
senin	sailor
kani	crab
kamome	seagull
shima	island
mōtā-bōto	motorboat
suijō-sukii	water skiing
mizugi	swimsuit
oiru-tankā	oil tanker (ship)
hamabe	beach
bōto	rowboat
oritatami-isu	deck chair
sakana	fish
roba	donkey
ashi-bire	flippers
tsuri-bune	fishing boat
mizu-kaki	paddle
ami	net
kaisō	seaweed
koishi	pebbles
rōpu	rope
kanū	canoe
fune	ship
gake	cliff
natsu no bōshi	sun hat
nami	waves
kai	shell

pages 28-29

gakkō	**school**
hasami	scissors
keisan	calculation
keshigomu	eraser
monosashi	ruler
shashin	photographs
fueruto-pen	felt-tip pens
gabyō	thumb tacks
enogu	paints
otoko no ko	boy
enpitsu	pencil
tsukue	desk
hon	books
pen	pen
nori	glue
chōku	chalk
e	drawing
doa no totte	door handle
shokubutsu	plant
chikyūgi	globe
onna no ko	girl
kureyon	crayons
sutando	lamp
iizeru	easel
buraindo	blind
kami	paper
suisō	aquarium
bajji	badge
arufabetto	alphabet
nōto	notebook
yuka	floor
kabe	wall
tenjō	ceiling
fude	brush
chizu	map
hako	box
sensei	teacher
gomibako	wastepaper basket
kokuban	board

pages 30-31

byōin	**hospital**
kangofu	nurse
dasshimen	cotton
kusuri	medicine
erebētā	elevator
gaun	bathrobe
matsuba-zue	crutches
jōzai	pills
o-bon	tray
ude-dokei	watch
taionkei	thermometer
kāten	curtain
gibusu	cast
hōtai	bandage
kuruma-isu	wheelchair
jiguzō-pazuru	jigsaw
isha	doctor
chūshaki	syringe
tedibea	teddy bear
ringo	apple
terebi	television
nemaki	nightgown
pajama	pajamas
orenji	orange (fruit)
isha	**doctor**
tisshu-pēpā	tissues
manga	comic
machiai-shitsu	waiting room
tsue	cane
omutsu	diaper
kādo	cards
nashi	pear
omocha	toys
kago	basket
budō	grapes
banana	banana
bando-eido	bandaid
konpyūtā	computer
surippa	slippers

pages 32-33

pātii	**party**
fūsen	balloon
chokorēto	chocolate
okashi	candy
mado	window
hanabi	fireworks
ribon	ribbon
kēki	cake
sutorō	straw
rōsoko	candle
kami-kusari	paper chains

omocha	toys
sandoitchi	sandwich
batā	butter
bisuketto	cookie
chiizu	cheese
pan	bread
tēburu-kurosu	tablecloth
denkyū	light bulb
ichigo	strawberry
ki-ichigo	raspberry
furūtsu-jūsu	fruit juice
sakuranbo	cherry
kasō-fuku	costume
poteto-chippusu	potato chips
sōsēji	sausage
kassetto-tēpu	cassette tape
sarami	salami
mikan	tangerine
purezento	presents

pages 34-35

omise	grocery store
gurēpu-furūtsu	grapefruit
ninjin	carrot
karifurawā	cauliflower
nira	Chinese chive
masshurūmu	mushroom
kyūri	cucumber
remon	lemon
serori	celery
apurikotto	apricot
meron	melon
tamanegi	onion
kyabetsu	cabbage
momo	peach
retasu	lettuce
saya-endō	peas
tomato	tomato
jaga-imo	potatoes
hōrensō	spinach
ingen	beans
reji	checkout
kabocha	pumpkin
tarorii	shopping cart
kanzume	cans
o-kane	money
saifu	coin purse
hando-baggu	purse
botoru	bottles

basuketto	basket
yōguruto	yogurt
pain	pineapple
niku	meat
bin	jars
hakari	scales
komugiko	flour
puramu	plum
tamago	eggs
kaimono-bukuro	carrier bag
chiizu	cheese
kudamo	fruit
yasai	vegetables

pages 36-37

tabemono	food
asa-gohan	breakfast
hiru-gohan	lunch
kōhii	coffee
yude-tamago	boiled egg
medama-yaki	fried egg
tōsuto	toast
jamu	jam
kōn-furēku	cornflakes
kokoa	hot chocolate
kuriimu	cream
gyūnyū	milk
satō	sugar
kōcha	tea
hachimitsu	honey
shio	salt
koshō	pepper
hotto-kēki	pancakes
rōru-pan	bread rolls
ban-gohan	supper
hamu	ham
sūpu	soup
omuretsu	omelette
hashi	chopsticks
sarada	salad
hanbāgā	hamburger
tori-niku	chicken
gohan	rice
sōsu	sauce
supagettii	spaghetti
masshu-poteto	mashed potato
piza	pizza
furaido-poteto	french fries
dezāto	pudding

pages 38-39

watashi	me
atama	head
kami	hair
kao	face
mayuge	eyebrow
me	eye
hana	nose
hoho	cheek
kuchi	mouth
kuchibiru	lips
ha	teeth
shita	tongue
ago	chin
ude	arm
hiji	elbow
onaka	tummy
mimi	ears
kubi	neck
kata	shoulders
ashi	leg
tsumasaki	toes
ashi	foot
hiza	knee
mune	chest
senaka	back
oshiri	bottom
te	hand
oya-yubi	thumb
yubi	fingers
watashi no yōfuku	**my clothes**
sokkusu	socks
pantsu	underwear
ranning-shatsu	undershirt
zubon	pants
jiipan	jeans
tiishatsu	T-shirt
sukāto	skirt
shatsu	shirt
nekutai	tie
hanzubon	shorts
taitsu	tights
doresu	dress
janpā	sweater
torēnā	sweatshirt
kādigan	cardigan
sukāfu	scarf
hankachi	handkerchief
suniikā	sneakers
kutsu	shoes

sandaru	sandals
būtsu	boots
tebukuro	gloves
poketto	pockets
beruto	belt
bakkuru	buckle
jippā	zipper
kutsuhimo	shoelace
botan	buttons
botan no ana	button holes
kōto	coat
jaketto	jacket
yakyū-bō	baseball cap
bōshi	hat

pages 40-41

hito	**people**
danyū	actor
joyū	actress
kokku	chef
kashu	singers
dansā	dancers
nikuya	butcher
keikan	policeman
fujin-keikan	policewoman
uchū-hikōshi	astronaut
daiku	carpenter
shōbōshi	firefighter
gaka	artist
saibankan	judge
seibishi	mechanics
biyōshi	hairdresser
torakku no untenshu	truck driver
basu no untenshu	bus driver
ueitā	waiter
ueitoresu	waitress
yūbin-haitatsunin	mail carrier
penkiya	painter
haisha	dentist
sensuifu	frogman
panya	baker
kazoku	**family**
musuko	son
otōto	younger brother
ani	older brother
musume	daughter
ane	older sister

imōto	younger sister
haha	mother
tsuma	wife
chichi	father
otto	husband
oba	aunt
oji	uncle
itoko	cousin
sofu	grandfather
sobo	grandmother

pages 42-43

dōsa	**doing things**
hohoemu	smile
naku	cry
kangaeru	think
kiku	listen
warau	laugh
uketoru	catch
nageru	throw
kowasu	break
egaku	paint
kaku	write
tataki-kiru	chop
kiru	cut
taberu	eat
hanasu	talk
horu	dig
hakobu	carry
nomu	drink
tsukuru	make
tobu	jump
hau	crawl
odoru	dance
arau	wash
amu	knit
asobu	play
miru	watch
noboru	climb
kenka-suru	fight
neru	sleep
toru	take
nuu	sew
haneru	skip
matsu	wait
ryōri-suru	cook
kakureru	hide
utau	sing
yomu	read

kau	buy
osu	push
hiku	pull
haku	sweep
tsumu	pick
fuku	blow
korobu	fall
aruku	walk
hashiru	run
suwaru	sit

pages 44-45

hantai no kotoba	**opposite words**
yoi	good
warui	bad
tsumetai	cold
atsui	hot
tōi	far
chikai	near
nureru	wet
kawaiteru	dry
ichiban-ue	top
ichiban-shita	bottom
kitanai	dirty
kirei	clean
ue	over
shita	under
futotta	fat
yaseta	thin
aku	open
shimaru	closed
chiisai	small
ōkii	big
sukunai	few
ōi	many
ichiban	first
saigo	last
hidari	left
migi	right
soto	out
naka	in
kantan	easy
muzukashii	difficult
kara	empty
ippai	full
yawarakai	soft
katai	hard
mae	front
ushiro	back

ushiro	back
takai	high
hikui	low
osoi	slow
hayai	fast
nagai	long
mijikai	short
kareta	dead
saiteiru	alive
kurai	dark
akarui	light
atarashii	new
furui	old
nikai	up
ikkai	down

pages 46-47

iroirana-hi	**days**
getsu-yōbi	Monday
ka-yōbi	Tuesday
sui-yōbi	Wednesday
moku-yōbi	Thursday
kin-yōbi	Friday
do-yōbi	Saturday
nichi-yōbi	Sunday
karendā	calendar
asa	morning
taiyō	sun
yūgata	evening
yoru	night
uchū	space
wakusei	planet
uchū-sen	spaceship
tentai-bōenkyō	telescope
tsuki	moon
hoshi	star
tokubetsuna-hi	**special days**
tanjōbi	birthday
purezento	present
rōsoku	candle
tanjōbi no kēki	birthday cake
tanjōbi no kādo	birthday card
kyūka	vacation
kekkon-shiki	wedding day
buraizu meido	bridesmaid
hana-yome	bride
hana-muko	bridegroom
kamera-man	photographer
kamera	camera
kurisumasu	Christmas day
santa-kurōsu	Santa Claus
sori	toboggan
tonakai	reindeer
kurisumasu-tsurii	Christmas tree

pages 48-49

tenki	**weather**
ame	rain
kasa	umbrella
kaminari	lightning
kiri	fog
taiyō	sun
sora	sky
kumo	clouds
yuki	snow
tsuyu	dew
kaze	wind
kasumi	mist
shimo	frost
niji	rainbow
kisetsu	**seasons**
haru	spring
natsu	summer
aki	autumn
fuyu	winter
petto	**pets**
hamusutā	hamster
morumotto	guinea pig
jūi	vet
inu	dog
inu-goya	kennel
ko-inu	puppy
esa	food
tenori-bunchō	budgerigar
ōmu	parrot
kuchibashi	beak
usagi	rabbit
kanaria	canary
torikago	birdcage
nezumi	mouse
ko-neko	kitten
neko	cat
basuketto	basket
gyūnyū	milk
kingyo	goldfish

pages 50-51

supōtsu to undō	**sports and exercise**
basuketto-bōru	basketball
bōto-nori	rowing
sēringu	sailing
uindo-sāfin	windsurfing
sunō-bōdo	snowboarding
tenisu	tennis
raketto	racket
american-futtobōru	American football
taisō	exercises
kuriketto	cricket (sport)
karate	karate
tsuri	fishing
tsuri-zao	fishing rod
esa	bait
ragubii	rugby
dansu	dance
yakyū	baseball
batto	bat
bōru	ball
suiei	swimming
tobikomi	diving, jumping
pūru	swimming pool
rēsu	race
ācherii	archery
mato	target
hanguraidā	hang-gliding
jūdō	judo
jogingu	jogging
jitensha	bicycle
rokku-kuraimingu	climbing
herumetto	helmet
batominton	badminton
sakkā	soccer
jōba	riding
uma	horse
ko-uma	pony
kōi-shitsu	changing room
rokkā	locker
takkyū	table tennis
aisu-sukēto	ice skating
sukēto-gutsu	ice skates
sukii	skiing
sukii-ita	ski
sutokku	ski pole
sukii-rifuto	chairlift
sumō	sumo wrestling

pages 52-53

iro	colors
cha-iro	brown
shiro	white
kuro	black
ao	blue
pinku	pink
daidai-iro	orange
hai-iro	gray
murasaki	purple
midori	green
aka	red
ki-iro	yellow
katachi	**shapes**
hishigata	diamond
daenkei	oval
kōn	cone
sankakukei	triangle
chōhōkei	rectangle
hoshi	star
seihōkei	square
en	circle
rippōtai	cube
mikazuki	crescent
kazu	**numbers**
ichi	one
ni	two
san	three
shi	four
go	five
roku	six
shichi	seven
hachi	eight
kyū	nine
jū	ten
jūichi	eleven
jūni	twelve
jūsan	thirteen
jūshi	fourteen
jūgo	fifteen
jūroku	sixteen
jūshichi	seventeen
jūhachi	eighteen
jūkyū	nineteen
nijū	twenty

pages 54-55

yūenchi	**fairground**
kanransha	Ferris wheel
merii-gō-rando	merry-go-round
suberidai	slide
matto	mat
wanage	ring toss
obake-yashiki	haunted house ride
poppu-kōn	popcorn
jetto-kōsutā	roller coaster
shageki	rifle range
gō-kāto	dodgems
wata-ame	cotton candy
sākasu	**circus**
ichirinsha-nori	unicyclist
akurobatto	acrobats
kuchū-buranko	trapeze
tsunawatari	tightrope walker
waiyā-rōpu	tightrope
pōru	pole
nawabashigo	rope ladder
anzen-netto	safety net
kyokugeishi	juggler
chōkyōshi	ring master
fūpu	hoop
inu	dog
usagi	rabbit
shiruku-hatto	top hat
bando	band
umanori	bareback rider
piero	clown
chō-nekutai	bow tie

This revised edition first published in 1995 by Usborne Publishing Ltd, Usborne House, 83-85 Saffron Hill, London EC1N 8RT, England. www.usborne.com
Based on a previous title first published in 1979. Copyright © 2002, 1995, 1979 Usborne Publishing Ltd.
First published in America in March 1996. This American edition published in 2003.